THE
REASON
for LIFE

ALSO BY
RICHARD E. SIMMONS III

THE POWER OF A HUMBLE LIFE
Quiet Strength in an Age of Arrogance

WISDOM
Life's Great Treasure

SEX AT FIRST SIGHT
Understanding the Modern Hookup Culture

A LIFE OF EXCELLENCE
Wisdom for Effective Living

THE TRUE MEASURE OF A MAN
*How Perceptions of Success,
Achievement & Recognition Fail Men in Difficult Times*

RELIABLE TRUTH
The Validity of the Bible in an Age of Skepticism

SAFE PASSAGE
Thinking Clearly about Life & Death

REMEMBERING THE FORGOTTEN GOD
The Search for Truth in the Modern World

THE
REASON
for LIFE

Why Did God Put

Me Here?

RICHARD E. SIMMONS III

The Reason for Life

Union Hill Publishing
200 Union Hill Drive, Suite 200
Birmingham, AL 35209

www.thecenterbham.org

1 2 3 4 5 6 7 8 9 10

Printed in the United States of America

TABLE OF CONTENTS

INTRODUCTION

....

T HE EARLY GREEK philosophers believed in a concept called the *logos*. It is where we get the English
word "logic." In Greek, the word *logos* literally means "the
word." However, it was also used in the world of philosophy and had the meaning "the reason for life." The
Greeks believed when one finds the *logos*, the reason for
life, they would be complete and whole. They will have
found their purpose.

The problem is that the Greek philosophers could
never agree on what comprised the *logos*. They never
seemed to be able to construct a unified belief on "what is
the reason for life?"

This has been a real problem for humanity throughout
the ages. We seek to find purpose and meaning in life,
only find it to be elusive.

I have written this book to help people answer the question; "What is the reason for life?" I will do this by seeking to answer a second pivotal question; "Why did God put us here?"

~ *Richard Simmons III*

CHAPTER 1

Life's Big Question

HAVE YOU EVER given much thought to the question: "What is the meaning of life? Is there a reason for my existence here on this earth?" When we get to the end of our lives, I believe we all would like to believe that our lives mattered and served a purpose of some kind

For many years now, I have enjoyed the writings of Dr. Peter Kreeft. He is an 81-year-old philosophy professor at Boston College who has written (by my count) 48 books, several of which I have read. In his book, *Making Choices*, Kreeft makes this observation:

> "*Every great philosopher has philosophized about it. Every great writer has written about it. And every active person has acted on it. It is the quest for the* summum bonum, *the greatest good, the ultimate meaning*

*and purpose of life, the answer to the question: Why
was I born? Why am I living?"*

Kreeft believes if we do not have a coherent answer to
this question, we will struggle to live a meaningful Life.

● ● ●

The prominent author and philosophy professor Dallas
Willard, in his book *Renovation of the Heart* states: "Meaning is one of the greatest needs of human life, one of
our deepest hungers—perhaps it is, in the final analysis,
the most basic need in the realm of the human experience. Almost anything can be born if life as a whole is
meaningful."

Willard goes on to say that "Meaning is not a luxury
for us; it is a kind of spiritual oxygen that enables our
souls to live."

Many people believe that Victor Frankl's classic
best-selling book, *Man's Search for Meaning*, is one of the
most influential books published in the United States.

Frankl, a prominent, Jewish psychiatrist and neurol-
ogist who lived in Vienna, Austria, was imprisoned in a
Nazi death camp during World War II. After he was released, he spent several years recovering and reflecting on
his experiences there. Frankl concluded that the difference
between those who lived and those who died came down
to one thing—meaning. He recognized that seeking to
find a meaningful life conflicts with a culture much more
interested in the pursuit of happiness. "It is a character-

istic of the American culture that, again and again," said Frankl, "one is commanded and ordered to be happy." However, he clearly realized that most adult Americans were not happy. His conclusion was based on the fact that most Americans do not realize that **happiness is the by-product of living a meaningful life.**

Further research in the social sciences demonstrates that living with a sense of purpose and meaning increases a person's overall well-being that includes life satisfaction, mental health, and self-esteem. Most significantly, a meaningful life decreases the chances of suffering from depression.

Having purpose in life, therefore, is a critical issue, but can we find a clear-cut answer to "What is the meaning of life?"

Is There an Answer?

Finding meaning and purpose is a question that reaches all the way back to Greek philosophers. As I mentioned in the introduction, they believed in a concept called the *logos*. It is where we get the English word logic. In Greek, the word *logos* literally means "the word," but it has a secondary meaning, "the reason for life." The Greeks believed that when one found his *logos*—his reason for life—he would be complete and whole, able to reach his full potential as a person. The problem is that the Greeks could never agree on what comprised the *logos*. As a result, they could never construct a unified belief on the reason for life.

• • •

When President Bill Clinton occupied the White House, he participated in a press conference aired on MTV. It was intended to be light and funny as he interacted with teens. Clinton was asked humorous, trivial questions such as, "What is your favorite rock group?" and "What kind of underwear: boxers or briefs?" But, out of the blue, 17-year-old Dahlia Schweitzer dared to ask a more thought-provoking question:

> *"Mr. President, it seems to me that Kurt Cobain's [lead singer of the rock group Nirvana] recent suicide exemplified the emptiness that many in our generation feel. What would you say to our generation about this?"*

President Clinton was visibly floored and did not know how to respond. He finally found an answer he thought suitable and basically told the young girl that everyone is important to each other in this life. There Schweitzer stood, asking the president of the United States to comment on the emptiness and meaninglessness of life that her generation faced, and one of the most influential men in the world did not have a relevant answer.

• • •

A number of years ago on the Oprah Winfrey Show, the host had a week-long series on "Answers to Life's Great

Questions." One of the shows was devoted to answering the question "What is the meaning of life?" Oprah apparently had several experts in her panel along with a large studio audience. Throughout the first segment, they did not come up with an answer. As they went to the commercial break, Oprah looked into the camera and said, "Stay tuned. When we come back, we are going to answer the question: What is the meaning of life?"

The same thing happened after each segment, with Oprah going into every commercial break saying, "Stay tuned for when we return, we are going to answer the question: What is the meaning of life?"

By the end of the show, no one coherently answered the question. With only fifteen seconds left, Oprah stared into the camera and said in conclusion, "Well, I guess you will have to look within yourself to find the answer."

With all due respect to Oprah, that was a pretty lame response. What she was really saying was, "I don't know the answer. If I had known I would have revealed it right here on live television."

● ● ●

So, what is the answer? As you examine your own life, can you find a good response to: "Why am I here? What is the reason for my earthly existence? What is the meaning of life?"

Furthermore, do you live with a sense of purpose? If not, perhaps it explains your struggle to find sustainable joy and happiness. For so many modern people, life does not make any sense, and they don't know why or what to do about it.

I plan to take the next chapter to look deeper into why we struggle so much to find meaning and purpose and then consider some helpful next steps.

CHAPTER 2

What is the Problem?

I BEGAN the last chapter with some words from one of Dr. Peter Kreeft's books. In another of his wonderful books, *C S. Lewis for the Third Millennium*, he makes an incredibly bold statement:

> *"We are the first civilization that does not know why we exist."*

Though he does not get more explicit, I assume he is referring to Western civilization, predominantly Europe and the United States.

He explains that the answers to the questions on purpose and meaning are all spiritual. He states that the essence of modern life has been the abandonment of our religious and spiritual foundations.

John O'Neil has served as president of the Californian School of Professional Psychology and consults with chief executive officers of major corporations. In his fascinating book, *The Paradox of Success*, O'Neil, who is clearly not a man of faith, shares insightful words about finding meaning in life:

> *"The basic questions we encounter when we look deeply into the shadow are spiritual questions. They concern our place and purpose in the world, the significance of our lives, and our personal connection to whatever force keeps the world humming along. Most of us today have moved away from the religious structures that once supplied answers to these questions, but the questions have not gone away. Our compulsive busyness, our dread of unstructured time, and our reluctance to be alone with ourselves are rooted in the uncomfortable sense that our lives lack meaning, that we are disconnected and alone."*

O'Neil is referring to the big questions of life, which he admits are spiritual, and says that they never go away but will always confront us. He shares that we have "moved away from the religious structures that once supplied answers to these questions," and asks, "Where does that leave us?" Disconnected and alone in the universe, with a life that lacks meaning.

When we seek an answer to where to find purpose and meaning in life, O'Neil is telling us that since our culture has abandoned the religious structures that have been foundational for so many years, we end up with no answers. If there is no God, we are here by chance and are nothing but a mass of molecules. We must conclude that a human life has no real value if we are nothing but a product of nature. If we are solely physical beings, we have no spiritual dimension to our lives. We live as meaningless beings in a random universe.

● ● ●

Why are we here? Again, if we live in a godless universe, there is no reason for our earthly existence. We are here by chance. Therefore, our lives are pointless because there is no God who endowed us with a purpose. To live with this worldview has to be quite troubling.

Dr. Armand Nicholi is a psychiatrist who teaches at Harvard Medical School. He has done a great deal of research on the life of C.S. Lewis. In his book *The Question of God*, he says Lewis believed the pessimism and gloom he experienced in his early life was clearly related to his atheistic worldview. He says that his conversion experience to Christianity changed his life filled with gloom and despair to one of joy, purpose, and many satisfying relationships. Life finally had meaning for him.

I think probably one of the most interesting books in the Bible is the book of Ecclesiastes. It is very philosophical, and most Bible scholars believe it was written by King Solomon, though the writer does not officially identify himself. It was written at a time in his life when he had abandoned God. As an old man, he was reflecting back on his life and referred to this period as "life under the sun," which means life from a mortal, earthly, finite perspective.

The book of Ecclesiastes describes his search for meaning without God. Solomon (who was, at the time, the richest man in the world) has had everything you could want in life, has done everything, and has tried every pleasure under the sun. In his own words he says, "I did not withhold any pleasure from myself."

In the end, he came up empty. He recognized that if there is no God that stands behind our earthly existence, then life is pointless. He says, "Life is meaningless, utterly meaningless," and describes finding meaning as chasing after the wind. Who can do it?

By the end of the book, Solomon came to the realization that we will never find meaning and purpose in life until we have some type of connection with what is above the sun. He is referring to life from an eternal, heavenly, perspective.

Solomon concluded that having a vertical connection with the divine changes everything about how we see and interpret life on the horizontal level.

Additional Insights

Solomon's conclusion is very logical. Purpose and meaning imply design. Your smart phone clearly has a purpose. It is not just a piece of plastic. It did not come into existence by itself or by accident. It clearly had a designer. Purpose implies design, and of course in order to have design, you must have a designer. When you consider a human being, his or her purpose is not as apparent and clear. For this reason, we must look to God, our Designer, to discover the answer to the questions:

What was I designed to do?
What is the purpose of my life?

We will look at the answer to these questions in the next chapter. However, I would add the idea that it seems only logical we function best as a human being when we do what we are designed to do. When we live apart from our design, we malfunction.

Author Tim Keller makes a great observation about the human desire for meaning. He asks the question, "If there is no God, and we are just finite beings, with no intrinsic value, and when we die and go into everlasting nothingness, then why do we yearn for meaning and a sense of permanence?" Where does this desire come from?

Keller says, "As you examine all of life, all of our innate desires have something that will satisfy them. There is no such thing as an innate, natural desire that does not have something that will satisfy it."

If you think about the desire of hunger, there is such a thing as food that will satisfy it. We all deeply desire to be loved, and there is such a thing as friendship, romance, and marriage.

C.S. Lewis said something very similar, "Creatures are not born with innate desires unless satisfaction for those desires exist." If this is true, then as we yearn and desire for a meaningful life, there must be something out there that will fulfill it.

CHAPTER 3

·····································

Why Are We Here?

THE BIBLE IS like a blueprint that provides a number of clues about our design, and when put together, we have a clear understanding of why God put us here.

In the book of Genesis, we are told several times (Genesis 1:26-27, and 9:16) that we are designed and made in the image of God. This means we possess a number of God's characteristics that none of His other creatures possess. For instance, we have a personality and emotions because He has a personality and emotions. He gave us the ability to think, reason, and be creative because He thinks, reasons, and creates.

We read in the Bible that God the Father, God the Son, and God the Holy Spirit have been in relationship with one another throughout eternity. The trinitarian God of the Bible is a relational God. For this reason, we too are relational beings. We thrive on relationships. In fact, if we were not relational beings, there would be no such thing as loneliness. I might add that loneliness is one of the plagues of modern life. Furthermore, the Bible is quite clear that we, as human beings, love others because God is a God of love. We are told that we have the ability to love because God first loved us. (I John 4:19)

• • •

There is a second clue about our design that helps us truly understand our reason for being here. A number of verses in the Bible, from both the Old and New Testaments, reveal this clue.

*Isaiah 43:21 "The people whom I **formed for myself** will declare My glory."*

*Colossians 1:16 "For by Him all things were created, both in the heavens and on earth, visible and invisible, whether thrones or dominions or rulers or authorities, **all things have been created through Him and for Him**."*

*I Corinthians 8:6 "...**and we exist for Him**, one Lord Jesus Christ."*

*I Corinthians 1:9 "God is faithful through whom you have been **called into fellowship** with Jesus Christ our Lord."*

God made us for Himself so that we would live in a meaningful love relationship with Him. It is the same reason parents choose to bring children into the world: we anticipate a lifelong relationship with them. The Bible describes this relationship as such: He is our heavenly Father, and we are to be His children. All of this explains Augustine's famous words: "God you have created us for Yourself and our hearts will not find rest until they rest in Thee."

The Apostle Paul tells us in Colossians 2:10, "In Him, (Christ) we are made complete." Through this relationship with Christ, we fulfill the purpose of our earthly existence and become complete as people. Conversely, to live without Him is to live without purpose and be incomplete, always searching for something to make us feel whole.

● ● ●

I remember watching a great illustration a number of years ago that can help us better understand this truth. A youth director wanted to illustrate to a group of teenagers what it means to be truly free. He got a goldfish bowl that was full of water and had a single goldfish in it. He proceeded to reach into the bowl, pick up the goldfish, and drop it on the table. The fish jumped two feet into the air and then off the table onto the floor. It flipped and flopped around for a minute and then lay still as its gills were straining for oxygen. The teenagers begged him to put the fish back into the bowl.

He protested and said to the students, "But the bowl is so confining; the fish is free outside of the bowl." He finally put the fish back into the bowl and explained that only in water could the fish be free to do what a fish does. And just as a fish is made for water, we were made for God.

What Are We Missing?

If this is how God designed us, why do more people not see and understand this? I think there are a number of reasons, but one reason in particular stands out to me.

Think about our desires, beginning with the desires of our bodies. We enter into this life with certain physical desires—we get hungry, thirsty, and tired. Then we hit puberty and our sexual desires kick in. These four desires of the body form the sensual side of life, and we have elevated these desires of the body to the point that they have become the center of our lives. For many of us, sensual pleasure (eating, drinking, resting, and having sex) provides the basic reason for living and has become the driving force in our lives.

Obviously, there is a proper place for these sensual pleasures since God has gifted them to us. Pleasure can bring great delight to our lives, but it does not give our life meaning or satisfaction.

However, many of us don't realize that we are more than a body that experiences sensual pleasure. We also have a spiritual dimension. We have a soul. Consequently, we have spiritual needs and desires as well. This includes our need for purpose and meaning, along with our desire for joy, happiness, and peace. These desires of our soul can only be satisfied by the Spirit of God. We all have a deep thirst in our souls for God and that thirst is satisfied by what Jesus calls "living water."

People today are attempting to satisfy the spiritual yearnings of their souls with the physical pleasures of life. However, it is not working, and it never will. The physical pleasures of life can never satisfy the spiritual longing of the soul.

C.S. Lewis put it this way in his book *Mere Christianity:*

"Over the centuries men tried to invent some sort of happiness for themselves outside of God, apart from God. And out of that hopeless attempt has come nearly all that we call human history – greed, poverty, selfish ambition, war, prostitution, classes, brutal empires, slavery – the long terrible story of man trying to find something other than God which will make him happy."

"The reason why it can never succeed is this: God made us, invented us as a man invents an engine. A car is made to run on gasoline, and it would not properly run on anything else. God designed humans to run on Himself. He Himself is the fuel our spirits were designed to burn, the food our spirits were designed to feed on.

There is no other. That is why it is just no good asking God to make us happy in our own way, without bothering to have a relationship with Himself. God cannot give us a happiness and peace apart from Himself because it is not there.

There is no such thing."

A Strange Encounter

I think one of the most interesting encounters that Jesus had was with the Samaritan woman at the well in John 4:7–19. She was drawing water and He asked her if He could have a drink. She was quite surprised that He, a Jew, would ask her, a Samaritan, for a drink since most Jews had no dealings with Samaritans. We learn that this woman has lived a troubled life and had been married five times and was at the time living with a man who was not her husband.

Jesus showed no condemnation towards her, only compassion. He lasered in on the spiritual need in her life and said to her: "If you knew the gift of God and who it is who says give me a drink, you would have asked Me and I would have given you living water."

She mistakenly believed Jesus was talking about some type of actual physical water that would make her life better and she replied, "Yes, give me a drink of this living water." He explained to her the problem with physical water was that she would thirst again.

The problem with the physical, sensual pleasures of life is that we look for them to satisfy us, but we always need more again. We can go to the finest resorts in the world, play on the top golf courses, eat at the best restaurants, drink the finest wine, and have the greatest sex, but we will wake up the next morning and find we are thirsty again.

Jesus then did something very perplexing. He asked her, "Where is your husband?" This would normally seem odd. However, Jesus understood that this woman had looked to sex, romance, and men to satisfy the thirst of her soul, but this approach to life had failed her miserably.

When we are looking for the things of this world to fill us and satisfy us, everything the world offers us is inadequate. We always get thirsty again.

New England Patriots quarterback Tom Brady was interviewed on CBS's "60 Minutes" after winning his third Super Bowl a few years ago. Along with his football success, he had plenty of other things our world values: fame, money, dates with supermodels. In fact, Brady had even married one. Yet, his interview revealed that something was missing.

"Why do I have three Super Bowl rings," Brady said, "and still think there is something greater out there for me? I mean, maybe a lot of people would say, 'Hey, man, this is what it is.' I reached my goal, my dream, my life. Me, I think, 'It's got to be more than this.' I mean, this isn't, this can't be what it's all cracked up to be."

When the interviewer asked, "What's the answer," Brady replied, "I wish I knew. I wish I knew."

It is hard to believe Brady had no sense of deep satisfaction after reaching his lifetime dream. In fact, he seemed surprisingly bewildered over the emptiness he experienced after this grand achievement. He must be wondering, *If this does not satisfy me, what will?*

● ● ●

In our innermost being, each of us has a deep yearning that seeks to be satisfied. Unfortunately, most of us are clueless as to what satisfies this strong desire. Countless types of pleasure, possessions, and achievements can attempt to provide it. But those things never keep their promise.

Jesus said, "I came that you might have life and that you might have it abundantly." He came to offer us living water that will satisfy this deep yearning of our souls.

A Final Story

C.S. Lewis demonstrates this truth very powerfully in one of his stories in *The Chronicles of Narnia*. The Narnia books are a series of allegorical children's stories, yet they speak powerfully into the lives of adults as well. A young girl named Jill, in Lewis' book *The Silver Chair*, presents a wonderful representation of humanity. She is clearly consumed with herself and is convinced that she alone knows what is best for her life. She wants to have nothing to do with Aslan, the great and magnificent lion who represents Christ. Yet Jill is desperately searching for water:

> *Jill grows unbearable thirsty. She can hear a stream somewhere in the forest. Driven by her thirst, she begins to look for this source of water—cautiously, because she is fearful of running into the Lion. She finds the stream, but she is paralyzed by what she sees there: Aslan, huge and golden, still as a statue but terribly alive, is sitting beside the water. She waits for a long time, wrestling with her thoughts and hoping that he'll just go away.*

Then Aslan says, "If you are thirsty, you may drink."

Jill is startled and refuses to come close.

"Are you not thirsty?" said the Lion.

"I am dying of thirst," said Jill.

"Then drink," said the Lion.

"May I – could I – would you mind going away while I do?" said Jill.

The lion answered this only by a look and a very low growl. And just as Jill gazed at its motionless hulk, she realized that she might as well have asked the whole mountain to move aside for her convenience.

The delicious rippling noise of the stream was driving her nearly frantic.

"Will you promise not to – do anything to me, if I come?"

"I make no promise," said the Lion.

Jill was so thirsty now that, without noticing it, she had come a step nearer.

"Do you eat girls?" she said.

"I have swallowed up girls and boys, women and men, kings and emperors, cities and realms," said the Lion. It didn't say this as if it were boasting, nor as if it were sorry, nor as if it were angry. It just said it.

"I daren't come and drink," said Jill

"Then you will die of thirst," said the Lion.

"Oh dear!" said Jill, coming another step nearer. "I suppose I must go and look for another stream then."

"There is no other stream," said the Lion.

• • •

I would ask you to honestly examine your life and answer these two questions:

- *What have you been chasing? What have you been looking at to quench the thirst of your soul?*

- *Secondly, how has it worked out for you?*

Jesus is quite clear: **there is no other stream.** There is no other source of living water. Everything we look to in this world never satisfies us, because we get thirsty again.

• • •

In the last chapter of the Bible, in Revelation 22:17, God gives each of us this invitation:

Whoever is thirsty, let him come, and whoever wishes, let him come and take the free gift of the water of life.

Will you take it? Will you drink? Or will you continue to fruitlessly look for some other stream?

CHAPTER 4

Putting It All Together

THE CENTRAL THEME of the Bible is man getting in right relationship with God. How does that come about? How does a person enter into a relationship with Him? To answer this question, I am going to lay out a short summary of the Bible.

Over the years I have shared this teaching with many people, and I cannot tell you how many of them have commented, "I have never heard this before." So many of these were churchgoing people who said they had never heard this message in their church. In fact, one man declared, "I think I am kind of mad about this."

It Starts with God

The famous Russian author Fyodor Dostoyevsky said, "My faith is not built on arguments of logic and reason;

it is built on revelation." He was observing that we could never figure out who God is as a Person unless He chose to reveal Himself to us in a way we would understand. This is what He has done, by sending the Old Testament prophets, the New Testament apostles, and by stepping into this world in the person of Jesus Christ as recorded in the Bible.

One of the most wonderful aspects of biblical revelation is that it reveals a great deal about who God is as a person, His nature, and His character. Though we could examine a number of passages, let's look at three.

- *I John 1:5*
  God is light and in Him there is no darkness at all.

- **Isaiah 6:3**
  Holy, Holy, Holy, is the Lord of Hosts. The whole earth is full of His glory.

- **Psalm 145:17**
  The Lord is righteous in all His ways and kind in all His deeds.

From these three verses, we can see there is no dark side to God. He is morally upright, perfectly holy, and righteous in all His ways. Dr. Ernest Gordon, the former chaplain at Princeton, described God as "the Word, the Principle, the Standard, the Norm of all morality in every age and place and civilization and university."

God has given us a moral standard to follow that are not arbitrary laws He pulled out of the air to impose on us. They are a reflection of who He is. He has always followed these standards because they are consistent with the holiness of His nature.

For instance, if you are ever asked, "Is there anything God cannot do?" you can answer, "Yes, the Bible tells us God is incapable of lying." He is committed to the truth and He is the truth. Therefore, being honest and truthful is part of God's moral standard.

God's laws fit our design, since we are made in His image. They serve as an owner's manual so that when we follow them, our lives flourish.

The Great Dilemma

So much more is revealed about God in the Bible, but let's turn our attention to the human condition. When we consider human nature, we see a stark contrast between Him and us. Some people believe in the inherent goodness of human beings, but this, however, is not the picture that is painted in the Bible. We are told:

- **Psalm 143:2**
  And do not enter into judgment with Your servant,
  For in Your sight no man living is righteous.

- **Isaiah 24:5-6**
  The earth is also polluted by its inhabitants, for they transgressed laws, violated statutes, broke the ever-

lasting covenant. Therefore, a curse devours the earth, and those who live in it are held guilty.

- **Jeremiah 17:9**
  The heart is more deceitful than all else and is desperately sick; who can understand it?

- **Romans 3:10**
  As it is written, "There is none righteous, not even one."

- **Romans 3:23**
  For all have sinned and fall short of the glory of God.

We are all sinners. We are all guilty and fall short of God's standard of perfection; and deep down, we all know it.

● ● ●

I do not think; however, we understand the depth of our sinfulness until we realize that God does not merely look at our words and actions but also the thoughts, motives, and intentions of our heart. For instance, in Matthew 5:28 men are told that if they lust after a woman in their hearts, they are actually committing adultery with her. Sinful thoughts in the sight of God are tantamount to sinful deeds.

Imagine God put a microchip in your brain that recorded your thoughts and the intentions of your heart for thirty days. Then He transcribed the recording and distributed it to all your family and friends. You would probably want to leave town for good.

Human Sinfulness

Sin in the sight of God is easily misunderstood. When the Bible speaks of human sinfulness, it is speaking of a natural condition of the heart—choosing to go our own way without reference to God. Pastor Howard Mumma says sin is "...putting God out of His central place in our lives and putting self in the center. Our will attempts to take the place of God. Sin is refusing to give God's place to God; we demand this place for ourselves."

Isaiah puts it this way:

"All of us like sheep have gone astray, each of us has turned to his own way."

● ● ●

One of the great Christian thinkers of the past, Augustine, recounts an incident from his teenage years. He and several of his friends climbed a wall and stole some pears out of an orchard. As he reflected back on this incident, he wondered why they did it. He realized it was not because they were hungry or poor. In fact, he really didn't like pears. So why did he participate in this act of stealing?

First, he realized it was because there was a sign that said "Keep out of orchard."

But then he began to realize, that deep in his heart there was a voice crying "My will, not thy will be done." "Thy" was everyone else in the world, including God. The primary intent of his heart shouted out: "My will be done." Furthermore, he recognized that at the root of every human heart is a voice crying: "My will be done."

This is our sin nature.

Augustine realized that this distorts everything in life, including all his relationships and all the decisions he would make. He concluded: my heart is desperately sick and sinful.

What do we learn from this story? We learn that it is our sinful nature that produces visible acts of sin.

One final point about our sinful nature is that we are born with it. Sin comes quite natural to us. Think about it—we do not teach our children to misbehave and be selfish; it comes natural to them. We inherit our sin nature from our parents, who inherited it from their parents.

● ● ●

Many years ago, when I was starting my career in the insurance world, I was sent to Hartford, Connecticut, for five weeks of training. I stayed in a small apartment and had a roommate from Peoria, Illinois. One night we got into a conversation about the human condition. He had believed all his life that mankind was inherently good. But one Christmas morning, his three- year-old son received a tricycle from Santa Claus. Later that morning the grandparents showed up and unbeknownst to the parents, they too gave the young son a tricycle. Since there were so many kids in the neighborhood who had no tricycles, the parents decided to keep both trikes. However, they stressed to their son the importance of sharing them with the neighborhood kids.

The next day, the father was watching his son out in the backyard with his Christmas toys and both trikes. He saw one of the neighborhood children come over and ask if he could ride one of them. To the father's disbelief, his son put a leg over one tricycle and a leg over the other one and told the other little boy to go home. The father was stunned because they had always taught the son to share (particularly his two tricycles).

He told me that this incident caused him to realize that we are not born with an inherent goodness, but that we are all naturally sinful.

● ● ●

A number of years ago, in a segment of "60 Minutes," Mike Wallace documented the story of infamous Nazi Adolph Eichmann. Eichmann, who had escaped post-war justice by fleeing Germany and remaining a fugitive for more than fifteen years, was finally captured and put on trial in the early 1960s. Wallace asked his viewers, "How is it possible for a man to act as Eichmann acted? Was he a monster? A madman? Or was he perhaps something even more terrifying: was he normal?"

Wallace followed this question with an interview of Yehiel Dinur, a concentration camp survivor who had testified against Eichmann at the 1961 trial. A film clip showed Dinur walking into the courtroom. He began to weep uncontrollably and then collapsed on the floor. Dinur explained to Wallace, "I was afraid about myself; I saw that I am capable of doing this. I am exactly like he." Eichmann was no longer that powerful Nazi who had helped orchestrate the Holocaust but rather simply an ordinary man.

As Wallace closed the segment he concluded, "Eichmann is in all of us."

So Where Does This Leave Us?

God is a perfectly holy God, and we are sinful, rebellious creatures who were designed to live our lives in relationship with Him. But there is a problem. We are told:

- *Isaiah 59:2*
  But your iniquities have made a separation between you and your God,
  And your sins have hidden His face from you so that He does not hear.

The heart of our problem is that we cannot have a relationship with God because our sin, our iniquities, have caused a separation between us and Him. A barrier exists between us. In Hebrews 3:10–11 we are told that because of our sin, we will not be able to enter into God's presence. In Romans 6:23 we are told that the wages, or consequence, of our sin is spiritual death—eternal, spiritual separation from God.

This spiritual separation is what the Bible calls hell. So many people struggle with the idea that a God of love would allow anyone to go to hell for all eternity. However, it is very biblical and is clearly confirmed by Jesus as being real. (I will address the issue of hell in Chapter 8.)

So, our sinful state keeps us out of relationship with God. Humanity by itself is not in right relationship with Him. Many people go throughout their entire lives separated from God, though they may believe He exists, they may go to church, and they may do religious things, but they are not in right relationship with Him. As a result, they are not experiencing the fullness of a relationship with a personal God who loves them and desires to live in fellowship with them.

It is critical to understand that God is holy and righteous, so it stands to reason that we need to be holy and righteous if we are to enter into His presence and be in relationship with Him. There are only two possible ways for this to happen. We can obey and follow God's law perfectly, or we can receive God's forgiveness and be cleansed from our sinfulness. The first option is not possible; the second is available to all of us.

Forgiveness of Sins

So, how are our sins forgiven? To fully understand this, we have to go back to the Old Testament and understand its system of sacrifices and the forgiveness of sins. From the very beginning, God required animal sacrifices because it was the way to demonstrate the severity of our sinfulness, the cost of our rebellion against God, and the death that sin brings. But most importantly, it represented the future sacrifice that Christ would make on the cross.

In the Old Testament the shedding of the blood of animals was necessary because God said in Leviticus 17:11 that He allows the blood of animals to make atonement for our sins. We are also told in Hebrews 9:22 that "without the shedding of blood there can be no forgiveness of sins."

These animal sacrifices made atonement for the people's sins. Atonement means to cover or cleanse. So, the animal sacrifices were a temporary means by which the people's sins were atoned for.

These sacrifices would take place during the course of the year; and in the fall of each year, there was a very special day on the Jewish calendar. It was called "The Day of Atonement," and is the most serious of all the Jewish holidays. Today the Jews call it "Yom Kippur." It was a day when no one worked and the people would spend much of the day fasting and in prayer, confessing their sins with great contriteness.

Two sections of rooms were located at the front of the Old Testament Tabernacle. The smallest of the rooms was called the Holy of Holies. A very thick curtain surrounded this room to bar entrance into it. The curtain reached from the very top of the temple all the way down to the floor. Access to this room was strictly forbidden except for:

- *One person – The High Priest*
- *On only one occasion – The Day of Atonement*

- *On one condition – He takes with him the shed blood of an animal.*

On the Day of Atonement, the High Priest would sprinkle the blood on what was called the mercy seat, and then he would immediately leave the Holy of Holies. He would not enter again until a year later on the next Day of Atonement.

However, we are told in Hebrews 10:4 that it is impossible for the blood of animals to permanently take away a person's sin; it was only temporary, until the day God would deal permanently with the sins of the world. I would remind you of the words of John the Baptist, spoken about Jesus as He approached John to be baptized:

- *John 1:29*
  Behold the Lamb of God who takes away the sins of the world.

The Ultimate Sacrifice

Many people are not aware that Jesus was born into humble means and spent His life as a humble carpenter until the age of 30. At this time, He began his public ministry that lasted a mere three years. In that three-year period, He never traveled far from Nazareth, His home. He taught in various communities, performed certain miracles, and poured His life into His twelve disciples.

Over time, the religious leaders began to resent Jesus. They did not like His teaching, they did not like the people He hung out with, and they did not like the manner in which He spoke to them. Most significantly, they hated the fact that so many of the Jewish people began to become followers of Jesus. They realized they needed to somehow get rid of Him, yet they could never seem to pull the trigger and have Him arrested.

And then an unbelievable event took place. Jesus raised Lazarus from the dead, a man who had been in the grave for four days. There were many witnesses present when Lazarus came walking out of the tomb. As you can imagine, the place erupted and many more began to follow Christ. It was at this point that these Jewish leaders began to plot with Judas on how to get rid of Jesus. They understood that if they did not act soon, the Romans would take away their high positions in this Jewish society.

Jesus was arrested at night and put on trial. He was eventually sentenced to death by crucifixion. However, before He was crucified, he was spat upon, mocked, and severely beaten.

The next morning, Jesus was crucified between two criminals at 9:00 a.m. Crucifixion was the most horrific form of execution ever conceived. In fact, by law no Roman citizen could be executed by crucifixion. Not only was it painful and torturous in that the one on the cross experienced excruciating pain for hours, but it was incredibly humiliating because the convicted person was stripped naked, hanging there for everyone to see.

For the first three hours that Jesus hung on the cross, He was mocked by many who passed by, while the Roman soldiers gambled for his clothes. Then He spoke to the two criminals who were crucified along side Him. He even prayed to God the Father: "Forgive them for they do not know what they are doing."

At twelve noon, darkness fell over the entire land. It was at that moment that God supernaturally poured all His wrath upon Jesus. Christ bore our sins in His body on the cross as He experienced all the condemnation and damnation that we deserve for our sinfulness and rebellion. God the Father had to turn away from Jesus because He could not be in the presence of the sin and evil Christ was bearing. It was because of this that Jesus cried out, "My God, my God, why have you forsaken Me?"

At 3:00 p.m., Jesus declared, "It is finished. Father, into Thy hands I commit My Spirit!" and died. At the exact moment of His death, the curtain in the temple tore from top to bottom (Matthew 27:51).

● ● ●

Dr. Tim Keller says in his book *King's Cross:*

> *"We must remember that the curtain in the temple was not a flimsy little veil; it was heavy and thick, almost as substantial as a wall. The curtain separated the holy of holies, where God's* shekinah *glory dwelled, from the rest of the temple—it separated the people from the presence of God. And remember that only the holiest man, the high priest, from the holist nation, the Jews, could enter the holy of holies—and only on the holiest*

day of the year, Yom Kippur, and he had to bring a blood sacrifice, an atonement for sins. The curtain said loudly and clearly that it is impossible for anyone sinful—anyone in spiritual darkness—to come into God's presence.

At the moment Jesus Christ died, this massive curtain was ripped open. The tear was from top to bottom, just to make clear who did it. This was God's way of saying, "This is the sacrifice that ends all sacrifices, the way is now open to approach me."

● ● ●

The best way to summarize all of this is to close with a few verses from scripture:

- ***Isaiah 53:5–6***
  But he was pierced through for our transgressions, He was crushed for our iniquities, the chastening for our well-being fell upon Him, and by His scourging we are healed. All of us like sheep have gone astray, each of us has turned to his own way, but the Lord has caused the iniquity of us all to fall on Him.

- ***I Peter 1:18–19***
  ...knowing that you were not redeemed with perishable things like silver and gold from your futile way of life inherited from your forefathers, but with the precious blood, as of a lamb, unblemished and spotless, the blood of Christ.

This final verse I have paraphrased so that we can fully understand what God has done for us:

- *I Peter 3:18*
  For Christ died once and for all (there are no other sacrifices necessary), the just (Jesus) died for us who were unjust, so that He might bring us into a relationship with God.

Remember, to live in relationship with God is why we are here and why we exist, but we could never have been able to have this relationship without the crucifixion.

CHAPTER 5

Seeking to Understand

A S I MENTIONED in the last chapter, there are so many people I encounter who do not understand the core message of the Bible. Yet understanding it is critical if we are going to properly respond to the Christian message and integrate it into our lives.

One of the most effective tools in my teaching is using stories and illustrations. Clearly Jesus believed this because He too used parables often to help His listeners better understand important truths.

In this chapter, I am going to share with you five short illustrations that will enable you to have an even better understanding of the core biblical message and what it teaches.

God's Great Rescue Mission

In Matthew 1:18-21, we read where Joseph has learned

that Mary is pregnant and he is not the father. We are told that he "not wanting to disgrace her, planned to send her away secretly." But then an angel of God appeared to him in a dream and said,

> *Joseph, son of David, do not be afraid to take Mary as your wife; for the Child who has been conceived in her is of the Holy Spirit. She will bear a Son; and you shall call His name Jesus, for He will save His people from their sins.*

Jesus' mission was established before He was even born. He came to save His people from their sins.

A word used several times in the New Testament by Paul that I think best captures what Jesus has done for us is the Greek word *rhuomai*, which literally means "to rescue and set free." Listen to Paul's own words:

> *For He **rescued** us from the domain of darkness and transferred us to the kingdom of His beloved Son in whom we have redemption, the forgiveness of sins (Colossians 1:13-14).*

In I Thessalonians 1:9–10, Paul says:

> *For they themselves report about us what kind of a reception we had with you, and how you turned to God from idols to serve a living and true God, and to wait for His Son from heaven, whom He raised from the dead, that is Jesus, who **rescues** us from the wrath to come.*

● ● ●

New York Times best-selling author of *Blue Like Jazz*, Donald Miller shares a great story in his book *Blue Like Jazz* about a rescue operation that took place several years ago in the Middle East. A team of Navy SEALs were performing a covert operation to free some American hostages.

"They flew in by helicopter and made their way to the compound and stormed the room where the hostages had been imprisoned for months. The room was filthy and dark. The hostages were curled up in a corner, terrified. When the SEALs entered the room, they heard the gasps of the hostages. They stood at the door and called to the prisoners, telling them they were Americans. The SEALs asked the hostages to follow them, but the hostages wouldn't. They sat there on the floor and hid their eyes in fear. They were not of healthy mind and didn't believe their rescuers were really Americans.

The SEALs stood there, not knowing what to do. They couldn't possibly carry everybody out. One of the SEALs, got an idea. He put down his weapon, took off his helmet, and curled up tightly next to the other hostages, getting so close his body was touching some of theirs. He softened the look on his face and put his arms around them. He was trying to show them he was one of them. None of the prison guards would have done this. He stayed there for a little while until some of the hostages started to look at him, finally meeting his eyes. The Navy SEAL whispered that they were Americans and were there to rescue them. 'Will you follow us?' he said. The hero stood to his feet and one of the hostages did the same, then another, until all of them were willing to go. The story ends with all the hostages safe on an American aircraft carrier."

Miller says that so many people see God as nothing more than an angry, judgmental, and wrathful God. However, he said that we should see Him more like these Navy SEALs, because He came to rescue us from His wrath. And Jesus does this by absorbing God's wrath on the cross.

Therefore, the decision to follow Christ is very much like the decision these hostages had to make to follow these Navy SEALs. I think we would all agree that it would have been a great tragedy if they had refused to follow them.

The Shedding of Blood

Jill Carattini, who works with Ravi Zacharias International Ministries shares a story and some commentary to help us better understand the shedding of animal blood for the atonement of sin.

She shares how for one family in Venezuela, the space between death and life was filled with more shock than usual. After a serious car accident, Carlos Camejo was pronounced dead at the scene. Officials released the body to the morgue and a routine autopsy was ordered. But as soon as examiners began the autopsy, they realized something was gravely amiss: the body was bleeding. They quickly stitched up the wounds to stop the bleeding, a procedure without anesthesia which, in turn, jarred the man to consciousness. "I woke up because the pain was unbearable," said Camejo. Equally jarred awake was Camejo's wife, who came to the morgue to identify her husband's body and instead found him in the hallway – alive.

Enlivened with images from countless forensic television shows, the scene comes vividly to life. Equally vivid is the scientific principle utilized by the doctors in the morgue. Sure, blood is ubiquitous with work in a morgue; but the dead do not bleed.

This is a sign of the living.

• • •

Thought and practice in Old Testament times revolved around a similar understanding – namely, the life is in the blood. It is this notion that informs the expression that "blood is on one's hands" when life has wrongfully been taken. There is a general understanding that blood is the very substance of our createdness, that in our blood is the essence of what it means to be alive. There is life in the blood; there is power.

The prophets sent throughout Israel's history were forever insisting that God wanted more than the empty performance of sacrifice. God desired these offerings to exemplify the heart of a worshiper, one who yearns to be fully alive in the presence of the creator. The blood of a living sacrifice made this possible temporarily, but God would provide a better way.

When Christianity speaks of Christ as the Lamb of God, it is meant to be a description that moves well beyond symbolism. Christ is the Lamb whose blood cries out with enough life and power to atone every sin, every shortfall, every evil and depravity of the world. He is the Lamb who comes to the slaughter alive and aware, on His own accord, and with His blood covers our deep need, moving us forever into the presence of God. There is life in the blood of Christ; there is power, and He has freely presented it.

How Good is Good Enough?

Bruce Wilkerson, a popular author, tells a very revealing story in his book *A Life God Rewards*. A woman he knew was concerned about her husband's spiritual well-being, and so she asked Wilkerson if he would meet with the husband. It is not surprising that her husband, Rudy, was not terribly happy about this meeting. Wilkerson tells the story this way:

> *I broke the ice by asking Rudy, "How may I be of help to you?"*
>
> *"My wife wants me to get religion," he said, scuffing the carpet with the toe of his shoe.*
>
> *I asked him why.*
>
> *He grimaced. "So, I don't go to hell."*
>
> *"Are you planning to go to hell sometime soon?" I asked.*

He looked at me, then burst out laughing. He seemed relieved to find that a Bible teacher might have a sense of humor.

"So, I continued, "when you stand before God, what's going to keep you out of hell?"

Dead silence, then Rudy chuckled. "I guess I never thought about it quite like that." He continued hesitantly. "I'm not a bad person, you know. I don't run around on my wife like some of my friends. And I choose to be a nice guy most of the time..."

I decide to help him out. "So, God probably has a big scale, wouldn't you think? On one side would be your sins – you do sin, don't you, Rudy?"

He nodded.

I continued. "And on the other would be all those good things you do for your wife, your kids, your community, and so on. Am I on the right track?"

Rudy nodded with more enthusiasm.

"And when God puts your life on His big scale, you'll have more good than bad, and everything will be okay, right?"

A smile crossed his face. He liked how my answer was shaping up. I told him that it all made sense to me, too, but I had a question. I took out my pen and drew a line like this:

TOTALLY EVIL   TOTALLY GOOD

|————————————————————————————————|

(0 percent good)   (100 percent good)

"Clearly," I said, "you just need to decide how much more good than bad you need for the scale to tilt in your favor." I handed Rudy my pen and asked him to put an X on the line to mark how close to Totally Good he'd have to get to be good enough for heaven.

Rudy studied my pad, then started to mark an X at about 60 percent. Then he reconsidered and moved it closer to 75 percent, then paused to think again. Finally, he shook his head and drew a rather feeble X at about the 70 percent spot.

He handed me the pen without looking up.

I pointed to his mark. "Let's say you hit your spot right on the nose, Rudy, because you really aren't that bad of a guy. But what if when you meet your Maker, He reveals to you that, unfortunately, the X spot is further to the right — say at 71 percent. If you were 70 percent 'good' but God said the minimum required score was actually 71 percent, where would a person like you go?"

Rudy crossed his arms and said, "It would not be good."

"Then finding out where the actual X is on that line would be the most important question of your life, right?" I asked.

Rudy grunted in agreement. "Yeah, but I am not too sure where it ought to be."

I closed my notepad and started picking up my things, but Rudy wasn't moving. "Can I know exactly where the X is?" he asked. "Cause I really need to know."

Wilkerson then showed him what the Bible says about that X. Rudy came to understand that God is holy and righteous; and in order to enter His presence, we also must be holy and righteous. Wilkerson explained to Rudy that we clearly come up short and that he could not be good enough to enter God's presence. He must receive God's forgiveness.

At the end of the day, when we eventually stand before God, the question is not going to be, "How good have you been?" The key question will be, "Are you forgiven?" Good people do not go to heaven; forgiven people do.

Understanding the Cross: A Parable

The heart of the Christian faith is the cross. Without it, the biblical story of redemption makes no sense. Therefore, to provide a good understanding of the cross, I share with you a wonderful parable from Dr. Norman Geisler, in his wonderful book: *I Don't Have Enough Faith to be an Atheist.*

The Judge

A young man is brought before a judge for drunk driving. When his name is announced by the bailiff, there's a gasp in the courtroom—the defendant is the judge's son! The judge hopes his son is innocent, but the evidence is irrefutable. He's guilty.

What can the judge do? He's caught in a dilemma between justice and love. Since his son is guilty, he de-

serves punishment. But the judge doesn't want to punish his son because of his great love for him.

He reluctantly announces the sentence: "Son, you
can either pay a $10,000 fine or go to jail."

The son looks up at the judge and says, "But, Dad,
I promise to be good from now on! I'll volunteer at soup
kitchens. I'll visit the elderly. I'll even open a home to
care for abused children. And I'll never do anything
wrong again! Please let me go!"

At this point, the judge asks, "Are you still drunk?
You can't do all of that. But even if you could, your
future deeds can't change the fact that you're already
guilty of drunk driving." Indeed, the judge realizes that
good works cannot cancel bad works! Perfect justice demands that his son be punished for what he has done.

So, the judge repeats, "I'm sorry, Son. As much as
I'd like to allow you to go, I'm bound by the law. The
punishment for this crime is $10,000 or you go to jail."
The son pleads with his father, "But, Dad, you know
I don't have $10,000. There has to be another way to
avoid jail!"

The judge stands up and takes off his robe. He walks
down from his raised bench and gets down to his son's
level. Standing eye to eye next to his son, he reaches into
his pocket, pulls out $10,000, and holds it out. The son
is startled, but he understands there is only one thing
he can do to be free—take the money. There's nothing
else he can do. Good works or promises of good works
cannot set him free. Only the acceptance of his father's
free gift can save the son from certain punishment.

God is in a situation similar to that of the judge—He's caught in a dilemma between His justice and His love. Since we are all sinners, God's infinite justice demands that He punish our sin. But because of His infinite love, God wants to find a way to avoid punishing us.

What's the only way God can remain just but not punish us for our sins? He must punish a sinless substitute who voluntarily takes our punishment for us (sinless because the substitute must pay for our sins, not his own; and voluntary because it would be unjust to punish the substitute against his will). Where can God find a sinless substitute? Not from sinful humanity, but only from Himself. Indeed, God Himself is the substitute. Just as the judge came down from his bench to save his child, God came down from heaven to save you and me from punishment. And we all deserve punishment. I do. You do.

The great mystery of the incarnation is that Jesus came into the world and was fully man and fully God. He had to be fully man so that He could be crucified on the cross. He had to be fully God to bear the sins of the world. Only God could do this.

Seeking to Understand God's Forgiveness

"It is finished."

Many people do not understand the significance of these last words uttered by Jesus as he hung dying on the cross.

Back in biblical times, like today, people would borrow money and incur debt. This seems to be part of the human condition. Since there was no elaborate banking system in that day, the common person might borrow from a wealthy individual. A written agreement, called a "certificate of debt" would be drawn up. This certificate of debt spelled out the terms and conditions of the loan.

Over time, if the debtor could not repay the loan (they did not have bankruptcy protection), the creditor had two options: He could have them sent to debtor's prison for a period of time which, in essence, would wipe out the debt. The preferred option would be to have the debtor work off the debt. In essence, the creditor owned the labor of the debtor. This may be where we got the idea of going to jail for a crime to pay your debt to society.

The Bible says this is the same situation we find ourselves in with God. As sinful people we have incurred a debt we can never ourselves repay.

Once the debt was paid off (through prison or labor), the creditor would take the certificate of debt and stamp it with the Greek word *Teleo*, which translates to "Paid in full."

When Jesus cried out "It is finished," the actual Greek translation is *Teleo*. Our sin debt is paid in full. Jesus suffered and died on the cross so that our certificate of debt, which consists of all our sins, could once and for all be "paid in full."

The Apostle Paul put it this way in Colossians 2:13-14:

God has forgiven us all our transgressions, having cancelled out the certificate of debt consisting of decrees

*against us, which were hostile to us, and He has taken
it out of the way, having nailed it to the cross.*

The redemption of a person's soul is costly, so much so
that we could never repay it ourselves. Only Jesus could
cancel it by the shedding of His blood. And in His last
dying words from the cross, He cried out, "Paid in full."

CHAPTER 6

My Response

THE NEW TESTAMENT divides people into one of three categories:

Non-believers
True believers
False believers

A non-believer is quite easy to identify. This person may or may not believe in God or Jesus. They generally have no interest in spiritual issues and no concern about their spiritual well-being. They generally are willing to acknowledge that they are not into religion and Christianity.

Being a true believer is what this book is all about. In these next two chapters we will consider what is a Christian, and if someone is not a true believer, how they can become one.

The final category, false believers, consists of people that Jesus was greatly concerned about. These are individuals who think they are in right standing with God but are not. They think they are Christians, but Jesus makes it clear they are not. This category is first addressed by Christ in the Sermon on the Mount in Matthew 7:21–23:

> *"Not everyone who says to Me, 'Lord, Lord,' will enter the kingdom of heaven, but he who does the will of My Father who is in heaven will enter. Many will say to Me on that day,*
> *'Lord, Lord, did we not prophesy in Your name, and in Your name cast out demons, and in Your name perform many miracles?' And then I will declare to them, 'I never knew you; depart from me, you who practice lawlessness.'"*

If you read this carefully you will notice that He is referring to people who think they are His followers but are not. He says that "not everyone who calls me Lord is going to enter into the kingdom of heaven," but the one who will enter must do so through the means God has provided. That's what He is referring to when He says: "He who does the will of My Father in heaven will enter."

He is making reference to the judgment seat of Christ. Notice He does not say that there will be a few false believers but "many." These people who had anticipated going to heaven are shocked when they find out they are not being allowed to enter. They argue with God. They speak of all the good works they have done and make it clear these works "were done in Your name."

False believers have a misunderstanding of what one must do to go to heaven. They believe that going to heaven is a result of believing in God and doing good works. They are sure that good people go to heaven and bad people do not. They do not realize that there are no good people; if you will remember, we are all sinners. As I said earlier, on the judgment day the question will be, "Are your sins forgiven?"

The mark of the true believer, on the other hand, is that they have a real relationship with God. They seek Him with the intent of knowing Him. In that last sentence quoted above, He is saying that because He never knew them personally, they should depart from Him. They are lawless sinners who have not received His forgiveness.

Christ speaks of false believers also in Luke 13:22-28.

"Then Jesus went through the towns and villages, teaching as he made his way to Jerusalem. Someone asked Him, "Lord, are only a few people going to be saved?"

He said to them, "Make every effort to enter through the narrow door, because many, I tell you, will try to enter and will not be able to. Once the owner of the house gets up and closes the door, you will stand outside knocking and pleading, 'Sir, open the door for us.' But He will answer, 'I don't know you or where you come from.' Then you will say, 'We ate and drank with You, and You taught in our streets.' But He will reply, 'I don't know you or where you come from. Away from Me, all you evildoers!'

There will be weeping there, and gnashing of teeth, when you see Abraham, Isaac, and Jacob and all of the prophets in the kingdom of God, but you yourselves thrown out."

Though this is a completely different setting and different words, Jesus again shared His great concern over false believers. In the end, He said, "I don't know you, or where you come from."

This is a very serious issue. Over the years I have seen men confronted by Jesus' words in Matthew and Luke, and it really has shaken up their lives. They concluded that Jesus was talking about them. As a physician told me, "I was a churchgoing family man, a good citizen, served humanity through my work, but I did not know Christ. Jesus' words in Matthew 7 hit me right between the eyes. I realized I was not a Christian."

● ● ●

The balance of this chapter and the next will answer the questions:

1. *How are we forgiven and cleansed of our sins?*
2. *How do we come to know Christ and have a real relationship with Him?*
3. *If I died tonight, how do I know for sure I would gain entrance into heaven?*

Are there any more important questions in all of life?

A Good Place to Start

I think a good place to start is with a verse most people are familiar with:

John 3:16
For God so loved the world, that He gave His only begotten Son, that whoever believes in Him, will not perish but have everlasting life.

Three chapters later, Jesus says:

John 6:47
Truly, truly I say to you, he who believes will have eternal life.

These verses both make it clear that you have to believe in order to have eternal life. In English the word "believe" is a friendly word. The big question is, what does it really mean to believe in Him?

● ● ●

Every time you see the word believe in the New Testament, it comes from the Greek word *pisteuo*, which means so much more that just believing something in my head. It means "believe in, to entrust, to rely on, to cling to."

Imagine you wake up one morning, you feel sick and know something is terribly wrong with you. You go to the doctor who then sends you to the hospital where they run a battery of tests. You are then told by the attending physician that what he has discovered is both good news and bad news.

The bad news is that you have a rare form of cancer, and if it goes untreated you will be dead within six months. The good news is that it is very treatable, and with proper chemotherapy there is a 100% recovery rate.

You breathe a sigh of relief because you believe what he has told you is true. But you need to do more than believe it in your head. True belief is completely entrusting your life into the doctor's care. It is completely relying on him and being willing to do whatever he instructs you to do. This is *pisteuo*. This is what it means to believe.

● ● ●

Another way of looking at this is to remember what we are talking about when we consider what it means to become a Christian. We are talking about entering into a relationship with Christ.

However, there is another relationship in this life. It is a holy relationship, and you have to enter into it as well. It is called Holy Matrimony.

I know some people find it odd that in four different places in the Gospels, Jesus is referred as the bridegroom. In John 3:29, John the Baptist refers to Jesus as the bridegroom. In Matthew 9:15, Mark 2:19, and Luke 5:34, Jesus refers to Himself as the Bridegroom, which explains why the church, the people of God, have always been referred to as the "bride of Christ."

The language used here—that of a bride and bridegroom—is the language describing a wedding where two people come together to be united in a holy ceremony. A wedding is one of the most significant events because we are entering into a whole new life.

Jesus uses the terms bride and bridegroom to demonstrate how we enter into a relationship with Him—a life-changing relationship. The next time you go to a wedding with a traditional ceremony, listen to the opening words:

> *"Dearly beloved, we are gathered together here in the sight of God and these witnesses, to join together this man and woman in holy matrimony, which is an honorable estate, instituted of God, **signifying the mystical union that exists between Christ and His church.**"*

The church has always recognized that marriage signifies and is a picture of what takes place between Christ and His people. Both relationships have to be entered into.

A Covenant Relationship

When people consider marriage, they will at some point count the cost of entering into this relationship. To many it means they are giving up being single, their independence, and their ability to make unilateral decisions. Everything they own becomes part of their spouse's possessions. It is a significant commitment, which is what God intended.

Marriage paints an accurate picture of what we must consider before entering a relationship with Christ. Many falsely believe they can become Christians with no real commitment on their part. They think they can serve Christ on their own terms. Jesus makes it clear we must completely entrust our life to Him if we want to be a true believer.

The next time you go to a wedding, pay close attention to the exchanging of the vows. In essence the bride and groom are giving themselves completely to each other. This is what must happen if you are to become a Christian. But know this, Jesus has already given Himself to us at the cross. Galatians 1:4, Ephesians 5:2. Ephesians 5:25, and Titus 2:14 all speak of Jesus giving Himself to us when He voluntarily laid down His life at the cross.

So, picture this: Jesus is the bridegroom and He is saying to each of us, "I have given Myself up for you, I have laid down My life for you. Will you receive Me, and will you completely entrust your life into My care? Will you surrender your heart? Ultimately, will you believe?"

This is the great question we all are faced with.

CHAPTER 7

....

Getting It Right

PROBABLY THE most well-known parable in the Bible is about a father and his two sons. Though we learn a great deal from the lives of both of these sons, I want to focus on the first son, the one that many call the Prodigal Son. We get a wonderful picture of how this son, who represents us and our rebellion, gets back into right relationship with his father (who represents God).

The parable is found in Luke 15:11–24. I will share the basic story and make comments along the way.

> *"A man had two sons and the younger son approached him and asked for the share of the estate that would one day be due him. Surprisingly, the father said yes. A few days later, the young son gathered all his wealth and possessions and traveled to a distant country. He then*

proceeded to squander his wealth on reckless and wild living.

This young son left his home looking for a better life, and he seemed to think he knew where to find it. He left with a real sense of freedom. I am sure he had the same attitude so many young people have today—they are bullet proof and are going out to conquer the world.

Most significantly, he wanted to get away from his father's presence. The young son wanted his father's money and financial support but did not really want anything to do with his father. This is so true of us. We want the blessings of God, but we just don't want God in our lives.

This young son did not want to live under his father's authority; he wanted the freedom to live however he chose to live. This, of course, is a picture of our sinful heart.

As the parable continues, the young son squandered everything he had and ended up with a job feeding pigs. No one was giving him anything. He was truly humbled, and I am sure he realized that he was not, in fact, bullet proof. His pursuit of the good life had broken down; and because his money was gone, no one around him seemed to really care.

We are told in the text that he finally came to his senses and recognized how lost he was. I am sure he also realized the cold hard fact that the world was not devoted to his happiness or well-being. He also recognized his true condition—he was dead and lost.

The parable goes on to say that the son finally recognized his need for his father. He was now able to see clearly and realized there was someone who loved him and cared for him. He knew his father at least would give him a job. However, in order to return to his father, he saw the need to do two essential things. Pay close attention to these two things because they are necessary for us to get into right relationship with God.

First, he recognized that he was a sinner and needed to confess his sins. The text says, "I will get up and go to my father, and will say to him 'Father, I have sinned against heaven and in your sight; I am no longer worthy to be called your son.'" The son recognized his need for his father's forgiveness, and he acknowledged his sin and asked the father's forgiveness.

The second realization the son had is that in order to get back into right relationship with his father, he had to leave his wayward lifestyle and return home on his father's terms. He could not go back on his own terms. The son was leaving his old life for a new one."

Unfortunately, what happens in the lives of so many people is they want to be a Christian but only on their own terms. A true believer is one who is willing to surrender their will to Christ and follow Him. It means turning our heart away from self and turning toward God. This is what the Bible calls repentance. It is to surrender.

We are by nature sinful human beings, wanting to live for self and be ruled by self. This is why we are called to repent and surrender.

We do not hear many people talk about or teach on repentance today. However, you would be stunned at the number of times it is mentioned in the Bible. Over the years, I have met with many men who are searching spiritually. At a certain point I have them read eight or nine verses that speak of repentance and I ask them in advance, before reading, "How important is repentance in becoming a Christian?" Most of them do not consider it to be important. We then read these verses:

- **II Peter 3:9**
  *The Lord is not slow about His promise, as some count slowness, but is patient toward you, not wishing for any to perish but for all to come to **repentance.***

- **Matthew 4:17**
  *(Jesus was returning from 40 days in the wilderness and was beginning His ministry.) From that time Jesus began to preach and say, **"Repent,** for the kingdom of heaven is at hand."*

- **Luke 3:3**
  *And he came into all the district around the Jordan, preaching a baptism of **repentance** for the forgiveness of sins;*

- **Luke 13:3**
  *"I tell you, no, but unless you **repent,** you will all likewise perish."*

- **Luke 13:5**
  *I tell you, no, but unless you **repent,** you will all likewise perish.*

- **Luke 24:45–47**
  *Then He opened their minds to understand the Scriptures, and he said to them, "Thus it is written, that the Christ would suffer and rise again, from the dead the third day, and that **repentance** for forgiveness of sins would be proclaimed in His name to all the nations, beginning from Jerusalem."*

- **Acts 3:19**
  ***Repent** therefore and return, that your sins may be wiped away, in order that times of refreshing may come from the presence of the Lord.*

- **Acts 17:30-31**
  *Therefore having overlooked the times of ignorance, God is now declaring to men that all people everywhere should **repent,** because He has fixed a day in which He will judge the world in righteousness through a Man whom He has appointed, having furnished proof to all men by raising Him from the dead.*

After reading these verses, I again ask the question, "How important is repentance in becoming a Christian?" The response I always get at this point is: "It seems to be essential." The dilemma comes when people realize that they believe in God and Jesus and want their sins forgiven, but they often are not willing to repent and surrender.

Repentance is an issue of the heart. It becomes a battle over who is going to rule over our heart. The Apostle Paul nailed our dilemma when he said:

- **Romans 2:5**
  But because of your stubbornness and unrepentant heart you are storing up wrath for yourself in the day of wrath and revelation of the righteous judgement of God.

C.S. Lewis says that what made atheism so attractive to him was that he could gratify his wishes and live however he pleased. This was also true of the young son in the parable.

However, when Lewis came to believe in God and recognized that Jesus was the Son of God who had died for his sins on the cross, it was only logical for him to surrender. It is like choosing to serve in the army of a powerful king. You do not negotiate with the king and tell him what you are willing to do. You bend your knee to him and serve him with your life.

In his book, *Mere Christianity*, Lewis says,

> *"Now what was the sort of "hole" man had got himself into? He had tried to set up on his own, to behave as if he belonged to himself. In other words, fallen man is not simply an imperfect creature who needs improvement: he is a rebel who must lay down his arms. Laying down your arms, surrendering, saying you are sorry, realizing that you have been on the wrong track and getting ready to start life over again, from the ground floor — that is the only way out of our "hole." This process of surrender — this movement full speed astern — is what Christians call repentance."*

Lewis is saying that the arrogance of man insists, "I belong to myself and I will run the show." The Christian humbles himself and declares, "I surrender and follow You."

The questions that only you can answer are: "Have you ever repented and truly surrendered your heart to Christ? Are you willing to follow Him?"

....

CHAPTER 8

A Choice Has
to Be Made

I SOMETIMES WONDER how well we know ourselves, particularly the deep thoughts and intentions of our heart. I do not think we realize how feelings, desires, and emotions have such a great influence on the decisions and choices we make. They often will cause us to bypass our logic and reason and lead us away from what is true. What I have concluded is that although our emotions and feelings may be real, they are unreliable.

As I work with people who are attempting to come to grips with the Christian faith, I often wonder what is going on in their innermost being. Are they being honest with me? Are they being honest with themselves? Are they being honest with God? Do they understand the tension that exists between the mind and the heart, and that this tension often paralyzes us and keeps us from following the truth?

One of the most wonderful examples that captures the essence of this human struggle to find Christ can be found in the life of Sheldon Vanauken. In his wonderful book, *A Severe Mercy,* Vanauken details his long spiritual journey. He first describes himself as an agnostic, but then later admits he was actually an easy-going theist who regarded Christianity as sort of a fairy tale.

Though Vanauken lived in various places in the world, he somehow struck up a long-distance friendship with C.S. Lewis. Much of the book is an exchange of letters between the two of them. In his letters, Vanauken would ask the spiritual questions that troubled him most, and Lewis would patiently and intelligently respond to them.

Vanauken describes the spiritual breakthrough that brought him to faith. Please take note of his thought process and how honest he is with himself:

"Christianity—in a word, the divinity of Jesus—seemed probable to me. But there is a gap between the probable and proved. How was I to cross it? If I were to stake my whole life on the Risen Christ, I wanted proof. I wanted certainty. I wanted to see him eat a bit of fish. I wanted letters of fire across the sky. I got none of these. And I continued to hang about on the edge of the gap."

At this point, he realized that he was in kind of a spiritual limbo. He described it in these words,

"The position was not, as I had been comfortably thinking all these months, merely a question of whether I

was to accept the Messiah or not. It was a question of whether I was to accept him—or reject. My God! There was gap behind me, too. Perhaps the leap to acceptance was a horrifying gamble—but what of the leap to rejection? There might be no certainty that Christ was God—but, by God, there was no certainty that he was not. If I were to accept, I might and probably would face the thought through the years: "Perhaps, after all, it's a lie; I've been had!" But if I were to reject, I would certainly face the haunting, terrible thought: "Perhaps it's true and I have rejected my God!"

"This was not to be borne. I could not reject Jesus. There was only one thing to do once I had seen the gap behind me. I turned away from it and flung myself over the gap towards Jesus."

A few days later he wrote these words to C.S. Lewis:

"I choose to believe in the Father, Son, and Holy Ghost— in Christ, my Lord and my God. Christianity has the ring, the feel, of unique truth. Of essential truth. By it, life is made full instead of empty, meaningful instead of meaningless. Cosmos becomes beautiful at the Centre, instead of chillingly ugly beneath the lovely pathos of spring. But the emptiness, the meaninglessness, and the ugliness can only be seen, I think, when one has glimpsed the fullness, the meaning, and the beauty. It is when heaven and hell have both been glimpsed that going back is impossible. But to go on seemed impossible, also. A glimpse is not a vision. A choice was necessary:

*and there is no certainty. One can only choose a side.
So, I—I now choose my side."*

The words of Vanauken that seem to be so pivotal are "A
choice is necessary." He is correct. A choice has to be made.

Accept or Reject

The moment of enlightenment for Vanauken was when he
realized that if he did not accept Christ, the alternative
was to reject Him. There are only two options. So, when a
person rejects Jesus, he is rejecting the One who came to
rescue him. In essence God is not sending this person to
hell; the person is choosing it.

There is a great true story that helps us understand
the choice we are all faced with:

*"In 1829 two men, George Wilson and James Porter,
robbed a United States mail carrier. Both were subse-
quently captured and tried in a court of law. In May
1830 both men were found guilty of six charges, including robbery of the mail "and putting the life of the
driver in jeopardy." Both Wilson and Porter received
their sentences: Execution by hanging, to be carried out
on July 2.*

*Porter was executed on schedule, but Wilson was
not. Influential friends pleaded for mercy to the president of the United States, Andrew Jackson, on his be-
half. President Jackson issued a formal pardon, drop-
ping all charges.*

Wilson would have to serve time in prison, but incredibly he refused to accept the pardon. An official report stated Wilson chose to "waive and decline any advantage or protection which might be supposed to arise from the pardon . . . "Wilson also stated he, ". . . had nothing to say and did not wish in any manner to avail himself in order to avoid sentence."

The authorities did not know what to do with him. They sent it to the courts, and it made its way all the way up to the Supreme Court. The U.S. Supreme Court determined, "The court cannot give the prisoner the benefit of the pardon, unless he claims the benefit of it . . . It is a grant to him: it is his property; and he may accept it or not as he pleases." Chief Justice John Marshall wrote, "A pardon is an act of grace, proceeding from the power entrusted with the execution of the laws . . . (But) delivery is not completed without acceptance. It may then be rejected by the person to whom it is tendered, and . . . we have no power in a court to force it on him."

*And so, they hanged him. **George Wilson chose to die.***

I find this story to be insightful because it reflects our standing before God. Every single one of us is in the same boat George Wilson found himself in. We are all guilty. As the Apostle Paul says, "We all have sinned."

The good news is that just like George Wilson, we have all received a pardon. When Jesus died on the cross, He bore our sins on His body. The Bible says that, "God caused the iniquity of us all to fall upon Him" (Isaiah 53:6).

Therefore, every single one of us has received a pardon for their sins. It is a gift of grace; it is nothing you earn. But as Chief Justice Marshall pointed out, the pardon is not complete without acceptance, and it may be rejected.

We all therefore must ask this question, "What have we done with the pardon God has granted us?" It is most critical to recognize the pardon is no good unless we have received it into our lives.

Not a Popular Message

The doctrine of hell is very unpopular, even in many churches ministers often refuse to teach on it. Modern people invariably seem to arrive at their beliefs not on the basis of what is true, but on what they find to be comforting and what makes them feel good.

The thought of being eternally banished from heaven and sent to a place of torment is not an attractive message. So many reject this doctrine, even though Jesus speaks more of hell than He does of heaven.

The following is a great illustration from Randy Alcorn's book; *The Grace and Truth Paradox*. It allows us to see that hell is logical and necessary if God is to carry out justice, remembering that justice is an essential part of God's very nature (Psalm 89:14).

"In the midst of a great and generous king's benevolent reign, he hears that some of his subjects have revolted. When he sends messengers to investigate, the rebels kill

them. So, he sends his own dear son, the prince. They murder him viciously, hanging his body on the city wall.

What would you expect the king to do now? Send his armies and take revenge, right? Kill those rebels! Burn their villages to ashes! *That king certainly has both the power and the right to avenge himself. But what if the king turned around and offered these criminals a full pardon?*

He tells them, 'I will accept my son, whom you murdered as the payment for your rebellion. You may go free. All I require is that you admit your transgressions, lay down your arms, live under my domain, and embrace my son's purchase of your forgiveness.'"

We'd be stunned—blown away—to hear this, wouldn't we? But the king is not finished.

"I invite any of you to come live in my palace, eat at my table, and enjoy all the pleasures of my kingdom. And I will adopt you as my own children and make you my heirs, so everything that's mine will be yours forever."

Incredible.

Then he says, "I won't force you to accept my offer. But the only alternative is spending the rest of your life in prison. The choice is yours."

Can you imagine someone responding, "How dare the king send anyone to prison? What a cruel tyrant"?

This is a picture of God's incredible grace and mercy. It is the gift of salvation that He offers to all people. How could anyone refuse this incredible offer? Paul says many reject it because of their stubborn and unrepentant hearts, and that they therefore are storing up God's wrath for themselves on the judgment day (Romans 2:5).

C.S. Lewis logically puts it this way:

> *"In the long run the answer to all those who object to the doctrine of hell is itself a question: "What are you asking God to do?" To wipe out their past sins and, at all costs, to give them a fresh start, smoothing every difficulty and offering every miraculous help? But He has done so, on Calvary. To forgive them? They will not be forgiven. To leave them alone? Alas, I am afraid that is what He does."*

Lewis goes on to say that "Hell is the greatest monument to human freedom. As Romans 1:24 says, '*God gave them over to their desires.*' All God does in the end with people is to give them what they want most, including freedom from Himself. What could be more fair?"

✿

Finally, I believe author Henri Nouwen in *The Freedom to Refuse Love*, has articulated a very logical understanding of God and the existence of hell. He says:

*"God is neither a policeman nor Santa Claus. God does
not send us to heaven or hell depending on how often
we obey or disobey. God is love and only love. In God
there is no hatred, desire for revenge, or pleasure in see-
ing us punished. God wants to forgive, heal, restore,
show us endless mercy, and see us come home. But just
as the father of the prodigal son let his son make his
own decision, God gives us the freedom to move away
from His love even at the risk of destroying ourselves.
Hell is not God's choice. It is ours."*

You Cannot Be Neutral

Jesus makes it clear that "He who is not with Me is against
Me" (Luke 11:23). There is no middle ground. You cannot
remain neutral towards Jesus. Choosing not to not make a
decision, in the end, is to make the decision to not accept
Him.

At a certain point in Jesus' ministry, He confronted
His own disciples with the necessity of a choice. In John
6:66–69, many of His followers began to withdraw from
Him and chose to no longer follow Him. They did not
like what He was teaching. He was standing there, with
only the twelve disciples remaining, and asked them, "Do
you not want to leave too and go with them?" Peter re-
sponded: "Lord, to whom shall we go? You have words of
eternal life. We have believed and have come to know that
you are the Holy One of God."

What a powerful response by Peter. If we do not put
our faith in Jesus, whom will we look to for eternal life?

In whom will we put our hope and faith? This is the question we are all confronted with. It is the choice we have to make. If we do not look to Christ for eternal life, to whom shall we look? Upon whom will we rely? Remember, faith must have a foundation, and if Jesus is not that foundation, who will be?

It is a choice only you can make.

What To Do?

Over the years I have gone through this material with various people. I have encountered many who quickly acknowledge they have never surrendered and put their faith in Christ. They want to know what to do.

Others are not certain if they are true believers and I tell them, "You can be sure." I ask them to think about marriage and entering into a marriage relationship. The bride and groom make vows by an ordained minister or priest.

In that same fashion I tell them that they need to make a similar vow to God through a prayer that I lead them in. I remind them that Jesus has already made His vow to us when He gave Himself to us at the cross.

So, if your desire is to enter into a relationship with Christ, to be forgiven of your sins, and to have eternal life, I ask that you humbly pray the following:

Lord Jesus,
I acknowledge I have tried to live life my way. I have disregarded You and Your will for my life. I acknowl-

edge that I am a sinful person and I pray that You would have mercy on me. I ask that You would cleanse me of all my sins.

And finally, I surrender my heart to You and seek from this day forward to follow You and Your will for my life.

I pray that You will come into my life and make me the man/woman that You desire for me to be.

I thank You for doing this!

In Christ's name,
Amen.

Moving Forward

I F YOU MADE the decision to enter in to a relationship with Christ, you need to know what this means going forward. It is so important to know that you have received God's forgiveness, which means you have received the promise of eternal life. One day, you will stand before the judgment seat of Christ, and you will not have to give an account of your sins because Jesus has accounted for them at the cross. We are now righteous in the sight of God.

Blessed are those whose lawless deeds have been forgiven, and whose sins have been covered.

Blessed is the man whose sin the Lord will not take into account. (Romans 4:7,8)

Furthermore, you have now been adopted into God's family. He is now your heavenly Father, and you are His child. You now have a relationship with Him, but it is up to you to pursue that relationship.

I want to share with you two important words that have great pertinence when it comes to our relationship with God. It comes from the last instruction that David gave to Solomon just before he died.

> *As for you, my son Solomon, know the God of your father,*
> *and serve Him with a whole heart and a willing mind; for*
> *the Lord searches all hearts, and understands every intent*
> *of the thoughts. If you seek Him, He will let you find Him;*
> *but if you forsake Him, He will reject you forever.*

The two words I would like you to focus on is **"know"** and **"seek"** and the connection between them. Starting with the word "seek," we must understand our ultimate responsibility as God's children is to seek Him with the intent of knowing Him personally. Our relationship with God will not be a living reality if we are not actively and daily seeking Him.

Below you will find some selected scripture from both the Old and the New Testaments that reveals our responsibility to seek God:

1. **Deuteronomy 4:29**
   *But from there you will **seek** the Lord your God,*
   and you find Him if you search for Him with all
   your heart and all your soul.

2. *I Chronicles 16:10,11*

   *Glory in His holy name; Let the hearts of those who **seek** the Lord be glad. **Seek** the Lord and His strength; **Seek** His face continually.*

3. *II Chronicles 7:14*

   *...if my people, who are called by my name, will humble themselves and pray and **seek** my face and turn from their wicked ways, then will I hear from heaven and will forgive their sin and heal their land.*

4. *II Chronicles 12:14*

   *He did evil because he did not set his heart to **seek** the Lord.*

5. *II Chronicles 15:2*

   *... and he went out to meet Asa and said to him, "Listen to me, Asa, and all Judah and Benjamin: the Lord is with you when you are with Him. And if you **seek** Him, He will let you find Him; but if you forsake Him, He will forsake you."*

6. *Psalm 27:8*

   *When You said, "**Seek** My face," my heart said to You, "Your face, O Lord, I shall **seek**."*

7. *Psalm 34:10*

   *The young lions do lack and suffer hunger; But they who **seek** the Lord shall not be in want of any good thing.*

8. **Psalm 63:1**

   *O God, You are my God; I shall **seek** You earnestly; My soul thirsts for You, my flesh yearns for You, in a dry and weary land where there is no water.*

9. **Psalm 105:3,4**

   *Glory in His holy name; Let the heart of those who **seek** the Lord be Glad. **Seek** the Lord and His strength. **Seek** His face continually.*

10. **Jeremiah 29:13**

    *You will **seek** Me and find Me when you search for Me with all your heart.*

11. **Amos 5:4**

    *For thus says the Lord to the house of Israel, "**Seek** Me that you may live."*

12. **Matthew 7:8**

    *For everyone who asks receives, and he who **seeks** finds, and to him who knocks it will be opened.*

13. **Hebrews 11:6**

    *And without faith it is impossible to please Him, for he who comes to God must believe that He is and that He is a rewarder of those who **seek** Him.*

From these verses we learn the following:

God is not obvious, He is somewhat hidden to us until

*we begin to **seek** Him. It is then that we will find Him. Also notice that as we **seek** God's face, we should notice that God is a person, a personal being. We are personal beings because we are made in His image.*

Finally, notice the promises that are made to those who seek Him:

1. *"You will find Him"*
2. *"They who **seek** the Lord will not be in want of any good thing"*
3. *"**Seek** Me that you may live"*
4. *"He is a rewarder of those who **seek** Him"*

We must all understand that God wants to be personal with us. He wants us to know Him. Read the following verses that address this issue of knowing Him:

1. ***Jeremiah 9:23,24***
   *Thus, says the Lord, "Let not a wise man boast of his wisdom, and let not the mighty man boast of his might, let not a rich man boast of his riches; but let him who boasts boast of this, that he understands and **knows** Me, that I am the Lord who exercises loving kindness, justice, and righteousness on earth; for I delight in these things,' declares the Lord."*

2. ***Jeremiah 22:16***
   "He pled the cause of the afflicted and needy; Then

it was well. Is not that what it means to **know**
Me?" declares the Lord."

3. **Jeremiah 24:7**
I will give them a heart to **know** *Me, for I am the
Lord; and they will be My people, and I will be their
God, for they will return to Me with their whole
heart.*

4. **Daniel 11:32**
*By smooth words he will turn to godlessness those
who act wickedly toward the covenant, but the people who* **know** *their God will display strength and
take action.*

5. **John 17:3**
This is eternal life, that they may **know** *You, the
only true God, and Jesus Christ whom You have
sent.*

6. **Philippians 3:8,10**
*More than that, I count all things to be loss in view
of the surpassing value of* **knowing** *Christ Jesus
my Lord, for whom I have suffered the loss of all
things, and count them rubbish so that I may gain
Christ.*

... that I may **know** *Him and the power of His
resurrection and the fellowship of His sufferings,
being conformed to His death.*

• • •

A Christian is someone who has entered into a relationship with Christ and then begins a lifelong journey of seeking God with the intent of knowing Him. It is the most important priority in life.

We seek God in the Bible. This is the way we hear His voice. It is in many ways a personal letter written by our heavenly Father to us.

He also desires to hear from us through prayer. He delights in hearing from us just as parents love to converse with and hear from their own children.

We can assist you in the "seeking" process by sending you material to help you.

Either go to our website:

www.thecenterbham.org

Or you can email me at:

richard@thecenterbham.org

Finally, it is important to be in a community with other Christians. It is important to seek out a good church if you currently don't have one. I would encourage you to find a men's or women's Bible study that you can regularly attend. You will find real strength in being in community with other Christians.

SOURCES

Alcorn, Randy. *The Grace and Truth Paradox*. Sisters, OR: Multnomah Publishers. 2003.

Frankl, Victor E. *Man's Search for Meaning*. Boston, MA: Beacon Press, 1959.

Geisler, Norman L., and Frank Turek. *I Don't Have Enough Faith to be an Atheist*. Wheaton, IL: Crossway Books, 2007.

Keller, Timothy. *King's Cross: The Story of the World In the Life of Jesus*. New York: Dutton. 2011.

Kreeft, Dr. Peter. *Making Choices: Practical Wisdom for Everyday Moral Decisions*. Ann Arbor: Servant Books, 1990.

Lewis, C.S. *Mere Christianity: An Anniversary Edition of the Three Books: The Case for Christianity, Christian Behavior, and Beyond Personality*. New York: Macmillan Publishing Co., Inc., 1981.

Lewis, C.S. *The Chronicles of Narnia, Book Six, The Silver Chair*. New York: Harper Trophy, Harper Collins Publishers, 1953.

Lewis, C. S. *The Problem of Pain*. New York: Harper Collins, 1996.

Miller, Donald. *Blue Like Jazz*. Nashville, TN: Thomas Nelson Publishers, 2003.

Nicholi, Dr. Armand M. Jr. *The Question of God: C. S. Lewis and Sigmund Freud Debate God, Love, Sex, and the Meaning of Life*. New York: Free Press, 2002, 115-116.

Nouwen, Henri. *"The Freedom to Refuse Love"*. Bread for the *Journey: A Daybook of Wisdom and Faith. New York: Harper Collins, 1996.*

O'Neil, John R. *The Paradox of Success: When Winning at Work Means Losing at Life: A Book of Renewal for Leaders*. New York: Penguin Putnam Inc., 1993.

Vanauken, Sheldon. *A Severe Mercy: A Story of Faith, Tragedy and Triumph*. New York: Harper One, 1977.

Wilkinson, Bruce. *A Life God Rewards*. Sisters, OR: Multnomah Publishers, 2002.

Willard, Dallas. *Renovation of the Heart: Putting On the Character of Christ*. Colorado Springs, CO: NavPress, 2002, 199.